Nuzzle

LOVE BETWEEN A BOY AND HIS SERVICE DOG

By Donnie Kanter Winokur
Designed and Illustrated by Jodee Kulp

Photography Wm Simmons, 4 Paws for Ability, Inc., Jodee Kulp,
Judy Mervar Kennels, Adair Kanter Barrett, Harvey and Donnie Winokur

**BETTER ENDINGS
NEW BEGINNINGS**
a voice for the voiceless

Minneapolis • Atlanta

©2011 Copyright
Empowered by Paws • Better Endings New Beginnings
Donnie Kanter Winokur • Jodee Kulp

WEBSITES:

www.BetterEndings.org
www.TheChancerChronicles.com
www.4PawsForAbility.org

EMAIL:

TheChancerChronicles@gmail.com

PUBLISHER:

Better Endings New Beginnings
6289 Brunswick Ave N
Brooklyn Park, MN 55429
763-531-9548

All rights reserved. No part of this publication may be reproduced, stored in a retrieval system, or transmitted in any form or by any means; electronic, mechanical, photocopying, recording, or otherwise without written permission of the Better Endings New Beginnings and Empowered by Paws, LLC.

Trade Paper	ISBN 13 — 978-0-9842007-3-3	ISBN 10 — 0-9842007-3-3
Trade Cloth	ISBN 13 — 978-0-9842007-8-8	ISBN 10 — 0-9842007-8-9
Create Space Ed.	ISBN 13 — 978-1-4664117-2-2	ISBN 10 — 1-4664117-2-4

*Dedicated to
Iyal's Pop Pop*

*who believes in
second chances
and gave us
the gift of
Chancer.*

My name is Chancer.
I am a golden retriever.

Right from the start my nose was my map!

My favorite place was ONLY a sniff away.

It was my Mommy.

She fed us ALL at the same time! It was crowded.

Mommy's name is Windy.
Daddy's name is Quinn.
As a puppy I drank—
**Breakfast, Lunch,
Snacks, and Dinner.**
Then I slept with my ten soft
warm brothers and sisters.
I didn't know who was who
or what was what.
Was my pillow a belly or a bottom?

It didn't matter because
I felt safe.

One day I woke up!
Goodness.
My back paws
    pushed up my bottom.
    My front paws
        pushed up my chest and head.

I felt BIG. **Oops.** I fell over.
I stood up. I stumbled. And I...

tumbled all the way
to Mom's
nuzzles and
kisses and
into...

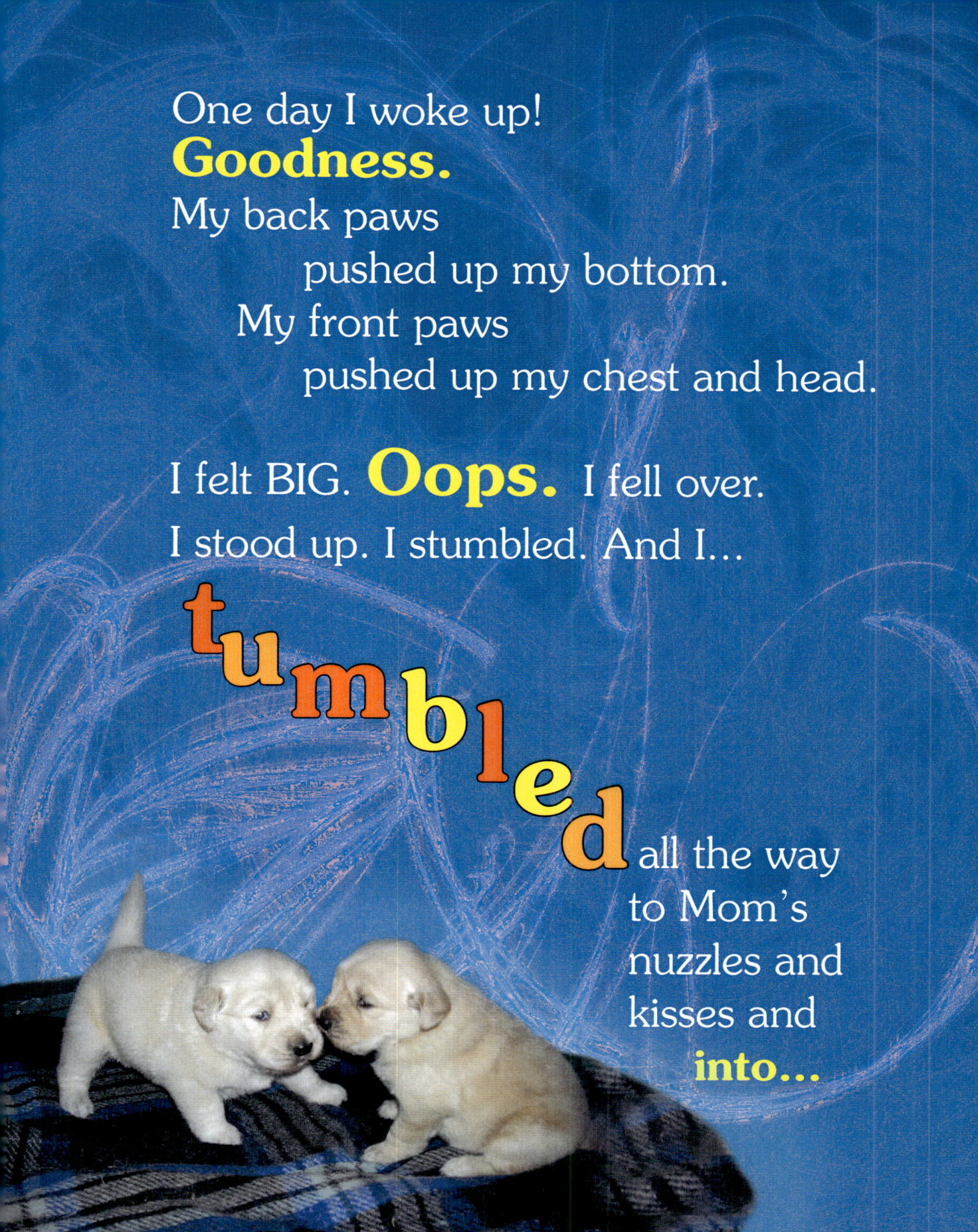

Puppy adventures!

Mom could **scent** when I was missing.
Her nose found me with
  nuzzles and love.
As I grew older
  I learned that dog smelling
    is called **scenting**
      in **People-Speak.**

Besides my smart nose
I have a shiny coat,
marshmallow heart and fluffy tail.

I love everyone!

When my heart feels joy

I jump and r-r-roof and spin circles.

This is my *Happy Dance!*

My heart knew
I was born to have a job.

I sensed this from the tips of my toes
to the whiskers on my nose.

I wanted to be...
    "a boy's fur-ever friend!"

I LIKED people.
I liked KISSING people.

Mom said in
Bow-Wow-Words
    "Be patient, Puppy.
       The day will come."

Soon a big white box
on wheels came.
Was this my boy?
I spun fast four times.

A lady's voice said,
"Let's buy him for our pet."

The man boomed,
*"He has to behave!
He needs to stay outside."*

Outside?
That didn't sound right.

Off we went in
the white box
on wheels.

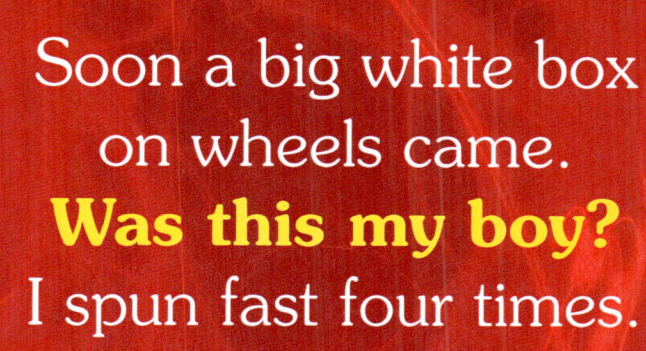

Bump.

We stopped moving.
I was carried to a yard
of new smells.
I wanted to spin with joy!
The lady reached down.

Aarf!

I got ready to kiss and lick!

But ... the lady hooked
my little collar to a **heavy chain**
stuck to a pole
in the ground.

"Bye for now,"
said the lady.

She walked away.

I tried to follow her.

"Please wait!"

I **pull-ll-ll-llled...**
but the chain
held me back.
The lady went into
a big blue wooden box.

The box didn't move.

It just stood
there.

And so did I.

I sat there for a **ver-r-r-r-y** long time!

It felt like

fur-r-r-r-ever!

The sun went down.

Night creatures said **"Hello"** to welcome me.

But I still felt

very alone,

until...

"Oh my!"
Where is that silly gurgling coming from?

I circled, looking behind me.
Mommy once said,
"Be still, watch and listen to solve a mystery."

I stiffened my hind legs.
I straightened my back.
I raised my head and **stood still**.

I didn't even pant.

My ears lifted, staying close to my head.
I "alerted!"
"Alerted" was People-Speak for how I stood.
It's how dogs pay attention.

Guess what?

I solved the mystery with my "Alert."

My tummy made that sound!

Then I got worried.
My eyebrows moved one at a time.
Taking turns, **up** and **down.**

Back and <-----> **forth,**
They did this when I was thinking.

Rrrrr that sound meant
I was hungry.

Rrrrreally hungry.

Where were the people to feed me?

Sniff WoOoOof sniff sniff.
My nose wiggled fast.
Kibble was coming!

I jumped side to side—
back and forth!

I wanted to be polite
and wait but…

I dove
nose first
into the bowl.
I didn't stop eating
until the last kibblet was gone.

I looked up to bark **"thank you."**
But the lady was gone.

I wanted to follow her.
But when my nose tried to
move my body closer—
the bad chain reminded
my neck it was stuck!
How could I say **"thank-you"**
...if I was **here** and
...she was **there?**
I circled three times and
plopped down to go night-night.

I was sad.

I did not feel like
part of this
new family.

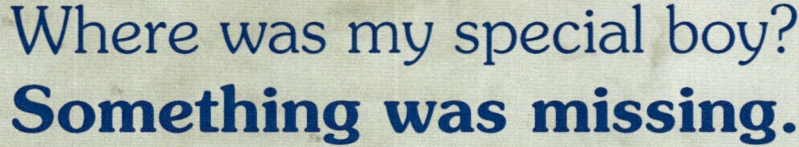

Where was my special boy?
Something was missing.

I thought about my mommy and…

I felt her love.

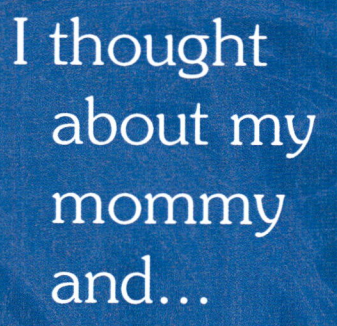

Her Bow-Wow-Words tickled my heart.

"Puppy, you will have a second chance!"

What did she mean and how did she know?

She's a mom.

Mom and Dad always woofed,

*"Tell the truth.
The truth never changes.
A made-up story
can be hard to remember."*

You never forget the truth.
So the truth is a lot of time went by.

It bothers me to tell you,
   but I became a year old.
That's seven years old in people years.

My puppy paws grew bigger.
My nose scented better.

**Still, I didn't feel like
part of a family.**

One cold day my nose woke up before the rest of me and… **"Kibble!"** My paws rubbed the sleepies from my eyes.

"Dog! We have a surprise," said the man.

I panted.

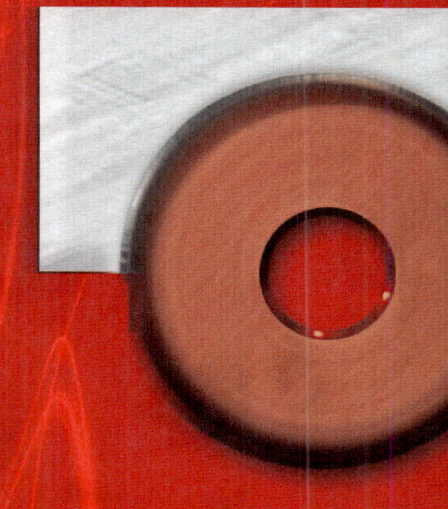

The lady said, **"You are going to a place filled with dogs."**

Faster panting!

"Friends are waiting for you."

I smiled as we drove away.

Bump. The door opened.
I knew this smell.
My paws hit the ground and started

the dance!
Squeallllllll
I was born here!
Smells became memories.

A lady named Judy hugged me.
"Look how you've grown!"
I snuggled against her legs.

...ooooO

I nuzzled into her goodness.
She rubbed my ears. **I was rescued!**

Then off I went in
another box with wheels.
Where were we going?

Bump again.
The door opened.
I smelled dogs EVERYWHERE!
My adventure started!

Inside, someone named Karen petted me.
"You're at 4 Paws for Ability. You are a very good dog and very special."

Was this the truth?

"And when you're trained you'll join a boy and his family."

My *Happy Dance* rippled my fur.
I smelled smiles!

Karen said, "Jeremy and Jennifer will train you. Your name is now **Chancer** and you have a **second chance**."

Their kind eyes showed they knew

Bow-Wow-Words!

"We have some friends to teach you **obedience**," said Karen. "You will go with another puppy and learn new skills."

So... *off I went excited to work hard* **and...**

do my job for my special boy.

I learned **"Sit"**
and **"Down"**
and **"Stay."**

When I did it right, I heard,
"Good Boy" and ate yummy treats.

I love
"Good Boys!"

When I earned enough **"Good Boys"**
I went back to 4 Paws for Ability.
Finally the **big day came**
to meet my special boy.

I was waiting in my kennel.
And it happened.
The latch moved.
I smelled their smiles
before I saw them!

Bright
faces
looked in.

**I smiled
really big!**

Here he was...
   my boy...
my special boy!

His name is Iyal
   and I call him **my favorite**.
   He was the reason I was born.
   He was adopted!
I hoped I could be too!

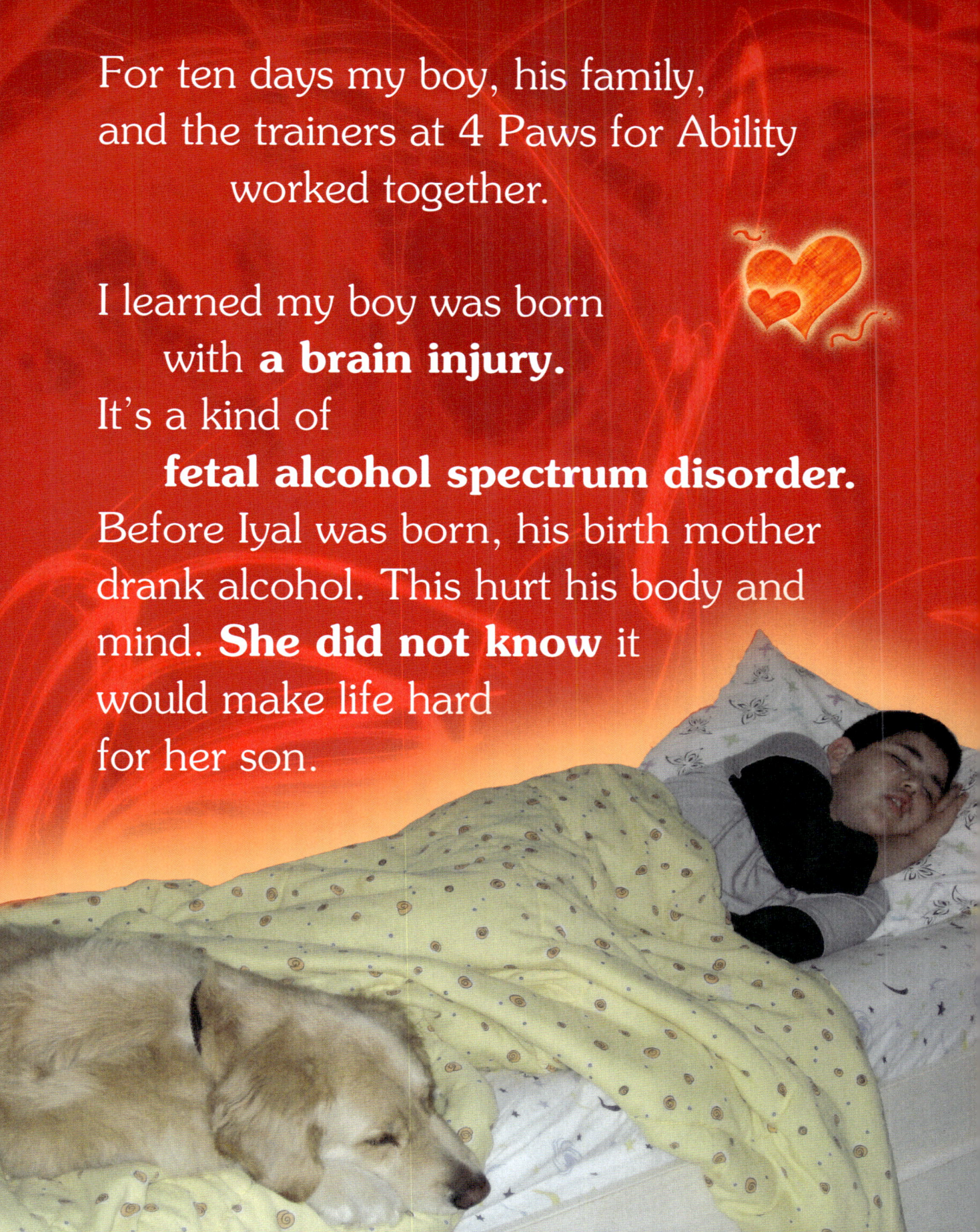

For ten days my boy, his family, and the trainers at 4 Paws for Ability worked together.

I learned my boy was born with **a brain injury.** It's a kind of **fetal alcohol spectrum disorder.** Before Iyal was born, his birth mother drank alcohol. This hurt his body and mind. **She did not know** it would make life hard for her son.

We worked really hard to learn together and **we were excited!**

It was graduation. We had to pass a test in the mall where we practiced.

If I followed the commands, my family could take me home.

Guess what?

Besides good people,
   my fur-ever home has cats.
   At first they were scared of me.
      As a service dog I am taught
      to sense fear.

Then they said, "meow."

I liked that!

Iyal's brain injury can make him scared of things he doesn't understand.

I comfort him by being as close as my fur lets me. But at times, he pushes me away.

"Go away dog!" my boy shouts. "Go away!"

I know he doesn't mean to hurt my feelings.

Deep inside…
   Iyal is just like everyone else.

   He loves with his heart.
      He is kind like you and me.
      He wants to do the right thing.

Iyal has to think really hard
  all the time.
And when he can't remember
  what the right thing is…
      Sometimes he gets scared.
      Sometimes he gets mad.
      And sometimes he stomps his feet.

When he is having a hard time
   he may make funny noises.

**But he always wants me
   back by his side.**

Sometimes if you
have an injury
in your brain
and you try
really really really hard
to do something...

It is just too hard!

It might look easy.
But it isn't for Iyal.

If my boy thinks
he is not good...
his heart breaks.
His mind spins around
and words twist out
of his mouth.

**It feels like our family
is in a tornado.**

I sense to stay near, but not too close. When the boo-boo storm is over my boy's face feels soft and colorful like a

RAINBOW!

I get up from wherever I am to find Iyal. His salty wet tears soak my fur.
"*I'm sorry, Chancer. I love you. You're my special dog*" ...*he sobs.*

I understand.

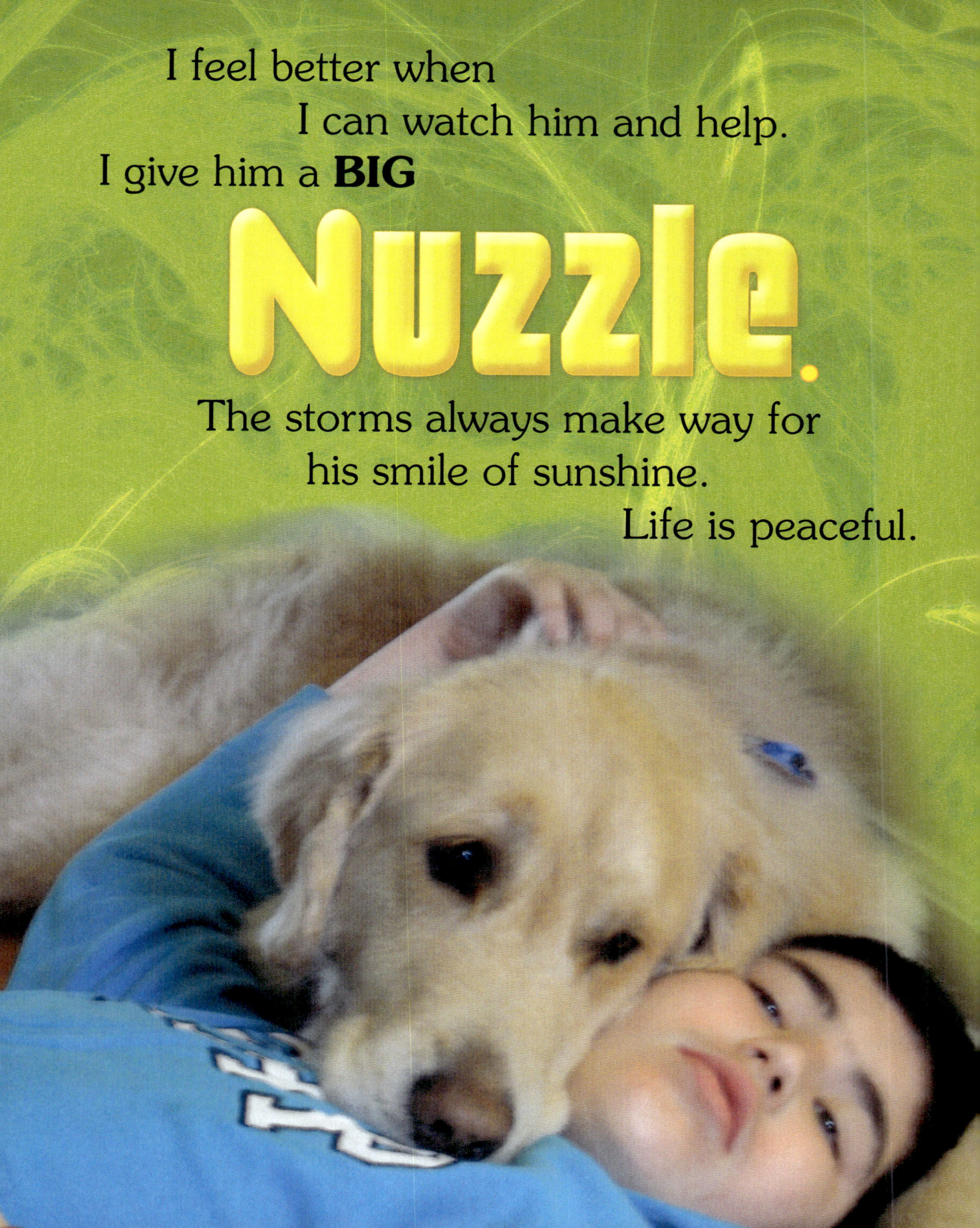

Shhh...

Here's a secret. Please don't ever **Woof!** this to anyone.

My absolutely, positively, cross-my-paws favorite command is

If my boy needs me
to nuzzle him...
I get to lick and kiss him.

This is my dream come true!
What an important job!

Sharing love is the best thing
in the whole wide world!

And sharing fun too!

Iyal's family takes me everywhere!

I shop at grocery stores.
I go to the doctor with Iyal.
I go to restaurants and go
"Under" the table.

I even go to temple and lie on Iyal's feet.

I am SO big

I take up five places on the floor.
Sometimes my family stands up to pray
and sits down to listen.
I look to see if
I need to stand.
I'm allowed to
pray lying down.

I am lucky to have a job that keeps my boy safe and feeling loved.

What could be better than a

Nuzzle.

by your fur-ever friend.

New words and ideas to talk about.

4 Paws for Ability: a training agency where I learned how to become a service dog.

Adopted: to become part of another family by law—like Iyal and me.

Alcohol: a beverage <u>only adults</u> can drink by law—such as beer, wine or liquor.

Birth Mother: the biological mother of a child.

Kibble: food I love to eat.

Nuzzle: when I use my love and kisses to help Iyal feel important and safe.

Obedience: things I learned like **"Sit" "Down" "Stay" "Come" "Under"** to do my job.

Scent: how I smell things.

Sense: using all my abilities to understand.

Service Dog: the name for a dog like me that helps people who are differently-abled.

What do I do for Iyal?

I am a service dog and I go everywhere with Iyal. I go to restaurants and temple. I even go shopping! My job is to help Iyal be calm and happy.

I'll tell you what kind of brain injury Iyal experiences…

The kind of **fetal alcohol spectrum disorder** Iyal lives with is called **fetal alcohol syndrome**. When he still lived inside his mom as an itsy bitsy baby she drank alcohol. She didn't know it hurt places in his brain and body. These injuries make thinking and learning hard for him.

Draw a picture of Chancer.

What did Chancer teach you?

Information about
Fetal Alcohol Spectrum Disorders (FASD)
(http://www.cdc.gov/ncbddd/fasd/data.html)

* We do not know exactly how many people have FASDs. CDC studies have shown that 0.2 to 1.5 cases of fetal alcohol syndrome (FAS) occur for every 1,000 live births in certain areas of the United States. Other studies using different methods have estimated the rate of FAS at 0.5 to 2.0 cases per 1,000 live births.[1]
* Scientists believe that there are at least three times as many cases of FASDs as FAS.[2]
* Prevalence estimates of alcohol use among women of childbearing age vary from state to state.[3]
* The lifetime cost for one individual with FAS in 2002 was estimated to be $2 million. This is an average for people with FAS and does not include data on people with other FASDs. People with severe problems, such as profound intellectual disability, have much higher costs. It is estimated that the cost to the United States for FAS alone is over $4 billion annually.[4]

References

1. Bertrand J, Floyd RL, Weber MK, O'Connor M, Riley EP, Johnson KA, Cohen DE, National Task Force on FAS/FAE. Fetal alcohol syndrome: Guidelines for referral and diagnosis. Atlanta, GA: Centers for Disease Control and Prevention; 2004.
2. Sampson PD, Streissguth AP, Bookstein FL, Little RE, Clarren SK, Dehaene P, Hanson JW, Graham JM Jr. Incidence of fetal alcohol syndrome and prevalence of alcohol-related neurodevelopmental disorder. Teratology 1997; 56(7):317-326.
3. Centers for Disease Control and Prevention. Alcohol use among pregnant and nonpregnant women of childbearing age – United States, 1991-2005. Morbidity and Mortality Weekly Report 2009; 58(19):529-532.
4. Lupton C, Burd L, Harwood R. Cost of fetal alcohol spectrum disorders. American Journal of Medical Genetics 2004; 127C(1):42-50.

SOURCES: Center for Disease Control's Fetal Alcohol Syndrome Prevention Team, Division of Birth Defects and Developmental Disability's, National Center on Birth Defects and Developmental Disabilities

BETTER ENDINGS NEW BEGINNINGS - HOPE FOR A BETTER FUTURE.

Pre-K Brain Stimulation Program
www.actg.org
Head Start/Preschool
Day Care/Homeschool

Elementary
Middle School

Middle School
High School

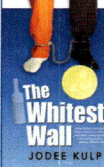
High School
College

College
High School

Teachers/Parents
College

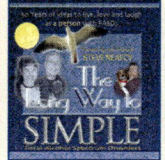
Teens/Adults
with FASD

Foster/Adoptive
Parents/Colleges

Young Adult
Adult

Creating voices for the voiceless — www.betterendings.org

NUZZLE – Love Between a Boy and His Service Dog

Iyal & Chancer

Nuzzle is a sensitive and humorous portrayal of adoption, disability and the unconditional relationship between a boy and Chancer, his service dog. Designed as an Early Reader for ages six and up, and told through Chancer's voice, this book will forever change the way you think about brain injury and second chances.

Readers will learn how this irresistible 90-lb. golden retriever helps to raise his special 'human' boy. Children and adults will understand the daily challenges faced by a child living with the lifelong, hidden birth defect called fetal alcohol spectrum disorder (FASD). FASD is the umbrella term used to describe a broad range of effects associated with alcohol use during pregnancy.

"NUZZLE is an auditory and visual joy—the lively artwork and engaging words offer an easy-to-read format both children and their parents will understand. How I wish I had such a book in my early journey into the world of FASD. Perhaps through the heart of Chancer, FASD can be better understood and families can receive the help they need most."

— Victoria Deasy, M.S. Special Education Teacher, California
  Consultant, Writer, Parent to a wonderful son with FASD

"NUZZLE is great and a beautiful way to teach children (and adults) about living with FASD. The illustrations are beautiful and it is so colorful. Congratulations on a wonderful publication!"

— Nancy Viking, Director of Development,
  NACAC (North American Council of Adoptable Children)

For more information on FASD, FREE curriculum, workshops and presentations visit:
www.BetterEndings.org and www.TheChancerChronicles.com

Read more about Chancer

Reader Views Kids 2010 Best Children's Book of the Year
Mom's Choice Gold Award for Outstanding Young Contributor

My Invisible World, Life with My Brother, His Disability and His Service Dog is written by Iyal's eleven-year-old sister, Morasha Winokur. She provides insight for middle school and early readers to understand and be more sensitive to peers who are differently-abled.